D1765765

THE WHITE MAGICK SPELL BOOK

Wiccan Spells for Healing, Blessing, and Protection

By Didi Clarke

Disclaimer:
While I have performed all these spells myself, your results may vary.

CONTENTS

*If you'd like to be notified when I publish a new book or have something exciting in the works, be sure to sign up for my mailing list. You'll receive a **FREE** color magick correspondence chart when you do! Follow this link to subscribe:*

https://mailchi.mp/01863952b9ff/didi-clarke-mailing-list

CHAPTER 1: THE TRANSFORMATIVE POWER OF WHITE MAGICK

Experiencing the power of white magick can be a life-changing event. Harnessing the spiritual energies of positivity, compassion, love, and healing is one of the best ways for a witch to be a force for good in her own life and the world at large.

And within the pages of *The White Magick Spell Book*, I'm going to show you how to do and be just that!

What You'll Find in This Book

I've done my best to make this a book that will benefit witches and other seekers and any point in their spiritual journey.

The book opens with an explanation about the basics of white magick—including the philosophies behind it, the tools a white witch needs, and the Gods and Goddesses associated with light and goodness.

Then we get to the really fun stuff—the magick itself! In the later chapters you'll find a wide variety of spells and rituals, including the following:

- Home Protection
- Emotional Healing
- Banishing Negativity
- Communicating with Guardian Angels
- Building Friendships
- And Much More!

Each of the spells you'll find in *The White Magick Spell Book* are broken down into easy, step-by-step instructions with plenty of explanatory notes to guide you through the process. It's important to understand the "why" of magick just as much as the "how."

However, it's my hope that these spells and rituals will help to expand the spiritual horizons of even the most experienced witch. They're all one-of-a-kind, original creations based on my own observations in the craft—you won't find these spells anywhere else!

Unlock the Power of Light in Your Own Life!

Are you ready to experience all the benefits that white magick has to offer? Then let's get started. Welcome to *The White Magick Spell Book*!

CHAPTER 2: WHAT IS WHITE MAGICK?

There are many different types of magick in the world of witchcraft that range on a spectrum from light to dark.

On the one side we have the dark or "black" magick. These are spells and rituals that have to do with blatantly dark things—revenge, violence, misfortune, invoking demons, etc.

But believe me when I say that this is not the path you want to go down. Black magick exists and really works, but when you bring darkness and pain into the world, you're inviting it into your own life too. Rituals can backfire and make your life a nightmare, but even when black magick does work correctly, there's no guarantee you'll escape unscathed.

Karma exists, right?

Towards the middle of our magickal spectrum, we have neutral or "gray" magick. This includes spells and rituals that are morally ambiguous, as well as those that don't have a large moral component to begin with.

For example, love spells would fall into this category. This type of magick is not actively harmful like a revenge spell would be, but there are still ethical concerns to consider (free will, etc.) that make it difficult to say with certainty whether it's right or wrong.

However, not all gray magick is questionable. Things like money or prosperity spells would be included in this group too. When you ask the spirit world for material wealth, you're not asking that other people be deprived of it, so there's no malicious component to this type of magick. But at the same time, asking for money is not a particularly noble aim of magick—you're not actively helping anyone, either. So, it falls within the category of gray magick.

Then we come to the subject of our book—white magick. This type of spellwork is all about actively drawing in goodness, peace, and protection into the world. Let's take a deeper look at what this entails.

Understanding the Purpose of White Magick

White magick (also known as natural magick or "the right-hand path") is all about making the world a better place. Some white magick spells are monumental and life-changing, while others are less extravagant in scope, but what joins them together is the desire of the practitioner to be a vessel for goodness and light.

There are a wide variety of white magick types that we'll discuss in this book, and some even seem contradictory.

For example, banishing negativity and bad energy is a form of white magick. But so is its opposite—drawing in positive energy. Once again though, if we look at the intent behind these different types of rituals, we'll see that they are one and the same.

White magick is also a practice of protection. Invoking deities or guardian angels (which I'll show you how to do) are two forms of this. Whether you're seeking protection for yourself or others, creating safety and assurance in the world is another goal in this type of witchcraft.

Spells of healing are another subgroup within white magick. Whether it's physical or mental, alleviating the suffering of others is one of the highest aims that a witch or any other person can aspire to, so it's no wonder this type of spell plays an essential role in white magick.

However, no ritual can replace the benefits of a professional doctor or therapist, so please don't think of white magick as an alternative to traditional forms of treatment.

But that being said, they can add another powerful dimension to our conception of health and healing.

Finally, many witches also include nature-based forms of magick (like herbs and potions) within the larger category of white magick.

This branch of witchcraft focuses on the oneness and unity of all life on the planet. We're all part of the unending cycle of the natural world, and the aim of plant magick it to bring it all into perfect harmony.

When phrased this way, it's obvious to see that nature-based spells fit well within our idea that all white magick has the intention of creating peace and goodness.

(If you'd like to know more about spells and magick that involve plants and the natural world, I highly encourage you to check out my book *Herbs for Witchcraft Volume 1*.)

Why Practice White Magick?

There are two primary reasons why a witch would want to practice white magick.

The first is perhaps a little less virtuous than the second, but it's important nonetheless—white magick brings good karma your way. Like I mentioned earlier in this chapter, bringing forth sadness and fear into the world makes you vulnerable to them as well. However, the opposite is true, too—bringing goodness in the world makes you more open to its effects as well.

Within the world of Wicca, there is a concept known as the three-fold law (or rule of three). This basically means that whatever you put into the world will return to you three times over. So, it makes pragmatic sense to practice white magick because you're basically increasing the likelihood that you will be rewarded for your efforts. Like I said—it's not the most virtuous mindset, but it is a smart one.

However, the real reason to practice white magick is a desire to make the world a better place. Whether you're a witch or not, all of humanity has to deal with this thing we call life, and making the process as easy as we can for one another is the least we can do.

You only have a limited number of days on this earth—would you rather spend them making life more bearable for your fellow human or would you rather spend it making all of us (yourself included) miserable?

To some extent, we're all born with a natural desire to practice compassion towards other living things. But you'll find that as you delve deeper into this branch of witchcraft that your compassion will begin to grow even more, until being a help to others is second nature. White magick has many practical benefits, but I think you'll find that the most important one is the transformation that takes place within your soul.

CHAPTER 3: WHITE MAGICK GODS AND GODDESSES

There isn't any set definition of what a white magick deity is, but if you study the Gods and Goddesses commonly found in Wicca and witchcraft, you'll begin to notice that many of them align with the principles of white magick.

In this chapter, I'm going to show you five different Gods and Goddesses that I associate with white magick. These deities all center around certain themes you find in the practice: life, protection, light, etc.

If you're looking for Gods to invoke as you journey deeper into white magick, these are the ones to call upon!

Baldur

In Norse mythology, Baldur is the son of Odin and the brother of Thor. Despite his fearsome family, this God is typically associated with joy, purity, and the sun.

During the summer solstice, witches typically honor the sun God, and for those who incorporate Norse deities into their practice, Baldur receives a place of honor at this celebration. He is viewed as a source of light, warmth, and protection.

Baldur is the God to invoke when you're trying to increase the happiness in your life. Your prayers to him won't magickally make all of your problems go away, but he is always ready and willing to point out the path to joy for a worthy seeker.

Brigid

Brigid is one of the most recognizable Goddesses of the Celtic pantheon. She was so popular, in fact, that when the Catholic church overthrew the traditional, Pagan religions of the region, the Goddess Brigid disappeared—but Saint Brigid took her place.

This powerful Goddess is associated with many different things by her worshippers, but for our purposes, I want to focus on Brigid as a life-giving healer and peacemaker.

In traditional mythology, Brigid was married to the Irish king, Bres. Though they came from different tribes that hated one another, she believed that the love between Bres and herself could unite the warring factions. While this eventually came to be, much hatred and bloodshed came before the peace.

After the death of her son, Ruandan, on the battlefield, Brigid's grief was enormous. Her mourning was so powerful that it caused both sides to put down their weapons and forge a peaceful existence with one another.

In other legends, Brigid was said to have healed lepers, and there are a number of magickal springs in Ireland that bear her name and are said to have mystical, healing properties.

Brigid is the Goddess you want to turn to when you feel caught in the middle of strife that you can't control. She brings peace to those who are mourning and healing to those in need.

Freyr

You might not be familiar with the Norse God Freyr, but you've almost certainly heard of his twin sister—Freya. But even though she might get the spotlight more than him, this deity still holds a place of importance in the Norse pantheon.

While he is most commonly associated with virility and childbearing, he's also known as the God of pleasure and prosperity. And unlike some of the more fickle, selfish deities, Freyr isn't just concerned with his own pleasure and prosperity—he freely and happily bestows it on his followers too.

Because of his associations with prosperity, it makes sense to invoke him in money magick, but that's not all he's good for. Any time you have a desire for personal fulfillment or spiritual prosperity, Freyr is around to lend a hand. He has the ability to help you self-actualize and reach your full potential.

As with all Gods and Goddesses, you should bring an offering when invoking Freyr. Some Gods only care that you bring them something of importance, but Freyr is specifically fond of baked bread and other handmade food items.

Ostara

Ostara is a Germanic Goddess of great importance within Wicca. She is commonly associated with the image of the Triple Goddess, our primary symbol of feminine divinity. And within this image, she takes on the role of the Maiden—the Goddess personified as a beautiful, youthful woman.

Because of these associations, Ostara symbolizes new life and purity. In fact, her principal celebration takes place on the spring equinox (sometimes itself called Ostara in honor of her)—which marks the rebirth or new life of the natural world.

In everyday life, Ostara is the Goddess to turn to when you're looking for a fresh start or want to rid your life of negativity and bad influences. Her life-giving power washes away the darkness of the past and provides you with a blank slate to create a better future for yourself.

Tara

Within Western witchcraft, Tara doesn't make much of an appearance. However, she is one of the most important deities in many branches of Hinduism. In fact, Tara is believed to be one of the oldest Goddesses in all of human history who continues to be worshipped to this day.

This Goddess has two primary incarnations that, while different, complement each other nicely.

First, there is White Tara, who is associated with healing and long life. She is considered the consort of the iconic bodhisattva Avalokiteswara and is said to have emerged from a lotus flower that bloomed where one of his tears fell.

Green Tara, on the other hand, is a Goddess associated overcoming obstacles and defeating adversity. She is seen as a protector of both the earth itself and her followers. Green Tara is the Goddess to turn to when your problems seem insurmountable and things feel hopeless.

CHAPTER 4: WHITE MAGICK TOOLS

In most magickal traditions, tools play a big role in performing spells—and white magick is no different.

In this chapter, I'm going to look at some of the most common items you'll want to keep around if you're serious about advancing in the art of white magick. Many of these tools will be useful for other types of witchcraft at well, but I've included them specifically in this book because of their association with banishment, blessing, and purification—three of the most important goals of white magick.

Please note that you should never begin using tools before they have been properly blessed or consecrated. You'll find a blessing ritual in the following chapter that can do just that!

Besom/Broom

What would a witch be without her broom (also known as a besom)? Even outside the world of Wicca, people associate brooms with witches—although we don't actually fly across the night sky with them!

Instead, a besom is traditionally used to cleanse a space both physically and spiritually. The physical aspect is pretty obvious—a besom sweeps up dust and dirt exactly in the same way that a mundane, non-magickal broom does. However, when blessed and consecrated as a tool of magick, a besom can take care of spiritual debris as well.

A modern-day broom can be repurposed as a besom, but I highly encourage you to construct one yourself. Traditionally, they are constructed by simply tying small twigs to a larger wooden staff or stick. They may not look all that impressive, but I think a traditional besom has a very nice, Old World charm to it.

If you have a place in your home where you regularly perform your spellwork, give it a sweep with your besom once a month during the new moon.

(To learn more about the phases of the moon and how they relate to magick, check out my book *Moon Magick of the Triple Goddess*)

This will clear your space of any negative energy, as well as any residual energy from previous spells—which can interfere with new spells in certain circumstances.

To cleanse the space, begin in the middle of the room and start sweeping in small, counterclockwise circles. As you sweep, repeat this:

The besom sweeps away the past to make way for the present. I banish all forms of negativity from this space.

Wand

While besoms push away negativity, wands can be used to do the opposite—draw in positive energy. Within the right context, a wand acts as a nexus point for spiritual energy to be harnessed and unleashed. This is not some silly toy we wave around; it's a conduit to the power of the spirit world itself.

Additionally, wands can also be used in the casting of a sacred circle, which is a preparatory ritual that witches use to seal and protect the space where they will be performing magick. Using a wand in this process can help to invite in positive energy and spiritual beings of goodwill.

At its most basic, a wand is nothing more than a branch from a tree. Each species of tree has its own unique magickal attributes, but oak and rowan are two good choices for witches interested in white magick—both have protective and healing properties.

Some people choose to adorn their wand with crystals, feathers, or other decorations. Additionally, there are lots of fantastic wand makers out there if you'd like something particularly fancy.

To select a wand, spend some time in nature communing with the trees. Allow your intuition to guide you to the wand instead of intentionally seeking it out with your rational mind. When you find the right branch, whatever you do, don't simply snap it off and run!

Trees are living, spiritual creatures just like you and I, so you've got to treat them with respect. To properly remove a branch for a wand, use a small knife to carefully and gently cut it. Once it has been removed, it's appropriate to leave a gift for the tree as a thanks for its sacrifice. I typically leave a small polished stone near the trunk or a bowl of consecrated water that I pour on its roots—however, always choose a gift that feels meaningful to you.

Quartz

Crystals can play an important role in witchcraft, and each kind has its own associations and correspondences. However, the type that's best for white magick is definitely quartz.

There are a number of different varieties of quartz available (amethyst, rose quartz, etc.), but I prefer to use plain, clear quartz because it seems to work best for storing and releasing Divine positive energy.

To charge your quartz with this Divine energy, it's as simple as allowing the quartz to sit under direct sunlight or moonlight. The sun is associated with the principal male deity within Wicca, so its rays will imbue your crystal with strong, active energy that invigorates and cleanses. On the other hand, the moon is associated with Wicca's primary female deity (the Triple Goddess), so it will charge your quartz with maternal, protective power. Both options are great for the working of white magick.

After your quartz has had time to sit in direct light (three hours at minimum), you can place it in a room in your home or carry it with you. A nice, large piece of fully charged quartz also makes a lovely and thoughtful housewarming gift for any witchy friends or relatives you may have!

Pentacle

A pentacle is a flat, round piece of wood or metal that has a five-pointed star (known as the pentagram) drawn, etched, engraved, or carved on the surface. It is used frequently in ritual magick (see my book *The Ritual Magick Manual* for more info), but it can also be used to banish negativity and bad spirits from a home or other place.

The easiest way to experience its protection is to hang it above your front door (on the inside or outside— your preference), but it's also fine to display it on a table or in some other creative way.

In addition to blessing your pentacle using the spell in the next chapter, you should also recite this short prayer immediately before you install it in your home:

The Divine spirit and the four elements meet in the points of this pentacle. May they work in harmony to protect, seal, and bless this place. So mote it be.

CHAPTER 5: WHITE MAGICK BLESSING RITUAL

L ike I mentioned in the last chapter, this blessing ritual is perfect for consecrating your magickal tools before use. However, that's by no means all it's good for!

This ritual is meant to be broad enough that it can be used for objects, places, or even people. Regardless of your intention, it will draw in positive spiritual energy that will cleanse and bless everything it touches.

We'll get into more specific types of blessings and invocations in the following chapters, but this particular ritual is a good introduction to the ins and outs of white magick. But don't let that fool you—this blessing ritual is just as effective and powerful as anything else you'll find!

Additionally, this blessing spell will introduce you to the four traditional elements found in Wicca and witchcraft—water, fire, earth, and air. We'll be invoking the unique powers of all four as the basis of our blessing.

If you're looking for ideas on how to incorporate this spell into your own practice, here are a few suggestions:

- Consecration of a new home
- Blessing paintbrushes, pens, musical instruments, or other creative/artistic tools
- Offering protection to a loved one going on a long trip
- The blessing of a new child

Really, when it comes to drawing in positive spiritual energy, there's no wrong reason to do it. Anyone and anything can benefit from a little magickal pick-me-up from time to time!

Preparing for the Ritual

This particular blessing ritual draws upon the Divine power of our moon, so it's one spell that should be performed after sunset, if at all possible. Specifically, you should aim for performing it during a full moon—this is the point of the month when the moon is brimming with purifying spiritual energy.

However, I'm a firm believer that you shouldn't let scheduling conflicts prevent you from exploring the world of magick, so don't be afraid to perform this ritual at another time, if the nighttime just won't work for you.

Regardless of when you perform the ritual, there is one preparatory step that will need to take place at night—but luckily, it doesn't require much effort on your part. You simply need to take a bowl of water and place it outside under the direct light of the moon. This will transfer the consecrating energies of the moon into the water itself.

Items Needed:

- Medium-sized bowl filled with water
- 1 white taper candle and holder
- Incense (any scent) and holder
- Small bouquet of wildflowers
- Matches

To begin with, you need to think about how to arrange your ritual space. If you're going to be blessing objects, they should be neatly arranged in the center of your area. Similarly, if you're going to be blessing a person, they should be standing or sitting in the center as well.

If you're going to be blessing a place, you might have to get a bit more creative. If it's a single room that you want to consecrate, simply perform the spell in that room. If you want a full house blessing, I would suggest performing the ritual in the entryway or living room—as they both symbolically represent the life and vitality of the home.

Start by walking a clockwise circle around your ritual area.

As you walk, repeat this:

This space is sealed with the power of Divine love and light. Only those of goodwill may enter its boundaries.

Move to the center of the circle, standing in front of your objects or the person. Pick up the bouquet of flowers and hold them upward and outward with both hands above your head.

Then say this:

Element of earth, bringer of stability. Through your power may we find protection.

Now, begin walking a smaller clockwise circle around whatever or whoever it is that you're blessing.

You should make three complete loops around them, and as you walk, repeat this:

I bless and consecrate this object/person with the power of earth. I ground it/them in the power of Gaia, our Divine earth mother.

Place the bouquet back down.

Next, light the candle and hold it in the same fashion as the bouquet.

As you do, repeat this:

Element of fire, bringer of vitality. Through your power may we find purification.

Once again, walk three clockwise circles around the object of your blessing while saying this:

I bless and consecrate this object/person with the power of fire. I encircle it/them with the ever-burning soul of the Universe.

This same process repeats for the incense.

Light it, hold it up, and say:

Element of air, bringer of hope. Through your power may we find peace.

As you walk your three circles, repeat:

I bless and consecrate this object/person with the power of air. I encircle it/them with the wings of the Divine.

Finally comes the water.

As you hold it up, you should say:

Element of water, bringer of regeneration. Through your power may we find new life.

One last time, walk three counterclockwise circles around your object or person while saying:

I bless and consecrate this object/person with the power of water. I encircle it/them with the majesty of the deep.

Unlike with the other elements, there is an additional step to be taken here. Place your right thumb in the bowl of water and use that to make a line across your object or across the forehead of the person being blessed.

Finally, stand once again before the person or object and repeat this final blessing:

I call the power of the four elements into this sacred place. Through your power all are blessed and made pure within the circle. To seal and protect is my will, and I make it manifest now. So mote it be.

After the ritual is over, your water should be disposed of outdoors.

If you were blessing magickal tools, no other steps need to be taken before they're ready to use. The power of this blessing ritual will remain imprinted upon them as long as they're used only for magickal purposes. However, if they are ever used for something non-magickal, they will need to be blessed again.

By Didi Clarke

CHAPTER 6: HOME PROTECTION RITUAL

The home is supposed to be a refuge from the troubles of the world. It's the place where you and your loved ones should feel safe and protected. When that feeling of safety is violated, it can throw our whole sense of self out of balance.

Whether you're worried about the physical or spiritual safety of your home, this protection ritual will help prevent unwanted negative influences from affecting you and your family. It acts like a counterpoint to the blessing ritual in the previous chapter—instead of inviting in positive energy, you'll be creating a seal around your home to prevent bad energy from making its way to you.

A word of warning before we begin—this spell (or any magick, for that matter) is not a substitute for sensible action. If you feel like you or your loved ones are in immediate physical danger within your home, please contact the authorities and take any other precautions needed to protect your safety.

Items Needed:

- 1 black taper candle and holder
- Matches
- Small bowl of salt
- Large hand bell

In a perfect world, this home protection ritual would be performed outdoors where you can circle the entire perimeter of your home. However, I'm well aware that there are many things that could prevent this from being a possibility. So instead, I would suggest performing it in one of your home's busiest rooms—like the living room. Performing it in an important room will symbolize that the ritual is intended for the entire house.

To begin with, clear your ritual space and stand in the center with your black candle. Light it and carefully raise it above your head with both hands.

As you do, say this:

I begin this seal of protection. I call upon the powers of the sacred Divine to banish all negativity and evil from this place.

Now, beginning at the southernmost point of the room, begin walking a counterclockwise circle with the candle around your ritual space.

As you walk, repeat this:

The circle turns, a defense is raised. I craft a wall of perfect power and light.

After this, return to the center of the circle and place the black candle down. Next, pick up the bell and return to the southernmost point of your circle. As loudly as possible, ring it six times—as six is a symbol for banishment.

After the last ring has ended, say this:

Spirits of the south, I call upon your aid. Seal this home and all within it from harm and wrongdoing. Set the spirit seal that none may break it.

Next, move to the west and repeat the ringing and invocation there (replacing "south" for "west").

Do this twice more—once at the north and once at the east.

To finish the ritual and complete the protective seal, return to the middle of your circle, put down the bell, and pick up your bowl of salt.

Once more, begin walking a counterclockwise circle around your space starting in the south. As you go, sprinkle some salt on the ground. You don't need to coat the floor, but sprinkle enough that it's at least visible—salt is one of the most powerful tools of protection used in witchcraft.

As you go, repeat this:

The seal is now complete. I call upon all beings of goodwill to enter and activate its power. May harm befall none that enter into this home. So mote it be.

To conclude, return to your candle and pick it up.

After extinguishing it, say this:

Though the circle is open, the seal remains. Let nothing disturb its protective power.

After the ritual is over, be sure to collect the salt you scattered and dispose of it outdoors, if possible.

The protective magick of this ritual should be slow to fade, but I recommend performing this spell once every one or two years. And it will need to be repeated in the event that you move homes.

CHAPTER 7: PERSONAL PROTECTION RITUAL

The next protection ritual I'm going to show you is meant to offer assistance, not in protecting a specific place, but a specific person. It can be performed either for yourself or a loved one.

Within this ritual, you will bless and assemble a talisman—which is a small object charged with magickal energy. Talismans can be used for a number of different purposes, and they're particularly useful when you want protection that will follow you wherever you go—it's as simple as carrying the object with you.

I know that I sound like a broken record at this point, but it bears repeating: this spell (or any of the spells found in this book) are not a substitute for taking practical steps to stay safe. If you feel like you are in immediate danger, I strongly urge you to take practical steps to maintain your safety and security.

The Protective Power of Obsidian

Obsidian is a beautiful, jet black stone that forms when lava from a volcanic eruption cools very quickly. This crystal (although it's technically known as "volcanic glass") has been used for millennia for both practical and spiritual purposes.

In the earliest ages of human history, obsidian was frequently used to create arrowheads and other tools, thanks to the nature of the stone—it's quite brittle, which means it can be broken into a sharp point. And, in fact, it's still used today to create super-sharp knife blades.

Magickally speaking, obsidian is valued for its protective and banishment qualities. Despite its dark hue, this is one stone that comes in mighty handy when working white magick! And that's why I suggest it for use as a talisman.

It's more than capable of deflecting bad energy—from others and yourself. Oftentimes, we humans are capable of generating plenty of anger and anxiety directed towards ourselves, but obsidian can help keep that self-negativity at bay.

Talisman Blessing Ritual

Items Needed:

- 1 piece of obsidian (small enough that it can easily fit in a pocket or purse)
- 2 equal lengths of white ribbon (to tie around the obsidian)
- 1 golden (or yellow) candle
- 1 silver (or white) candle
- Matches or lighter
- 1 handheld mirror

To begin the ritual, clear your workspace and light the gold and silver candles. These represent the Lord and Lady—the two primary deities of Wicca.

Repeat the following to invoke them:

Great Lord and Lady—our father, the bright Horned God, our mother, the radiant Triple Goddess—I call you down into this place. Parents of all humanity, I ask for your assistance and paternal protection. Bless these objects that they may create peace and safety for any and all who bear them.

Now, pick up the obsidian and hold it above the flames.

While you do this, repeat the following:

The power of obsidian obliterates all negative energy. Darkness repelling darkness.

Now, place the obsidian back down and pick up the white ribbons. Hold them over the flames as well.

Then, say this:

The strands of pure brightness hold back all evil entities. The light of righteousness dispels all sorrow.

Now, take one of the ribbons and tie it across the obsidian. When preparing for this ritual, double check to ensure that the ribbons are long enough to do so!

After one has been tied, place the other one at a 90-degree angle and tie it to create a cross. While the cross is typically associated with Christianity, its history predates the religion—the cross has been used by numerous societies and religions as a symbol of protection and banishment.

Once the tying is complete, hold your finished talisman over the flames once more.

This time, say this:

The talisman is complete and ready to protect the carrier.

Next, take your mirror and position it so that the light of the candle flames reflect onto the talisman. This will charge it with the power of the Lord and Lady.

Allow it to charge for a moment before continuing the ritual with these words:

The power of the great God and wise Goddess completes my act. May your protective power charge my talisman for good and light. So mote it be.

To finish the ritual, extinguish your candles.

Once the ritual is complete, your talisman is fully charged, blessed, and ready to use. If it will be used for yourself, simply slip it in your pocket or bag wherever you go to experience its protective power. If you plan on giving it to a friend or loved one, try to plan the gift giving for a special occasion (like a birthday). Choosing a significant time will help to increase the goodness and positivity that the talisman embodies.

CHAPTER 8: WHITE MAGICK BANISHING RITUAL

Even though we can't see it with our eyes, the spiritual energy that manifests itself in a given location has an effect on our emotional and physical wellbeing. When a place has good energy, we're more likely to feel positive, upbeat, and hopeful. But if a place has bad energy, it can lead us to feelings of anger, anxiety, jealousy, and a number of other negative emotions.

The spell I'm going to show you in this chapter will help to eliminate negative energy from a place and banish for good. It involves the art of smudging—which has been used for centuries to cleanse and consecrate spaces.

What Causes Bad Energy?

There are a number of possible reasons that negative spiritual energy can begin to accumulate in a particular place.

Sites of violence or extreme distress are prone to bad energy because of the psychic wounds that violent acts cause. Even though time may fade the memories of terrible things, like murder, the negativity, fear, and pain that is produced by such acts tends to stick around for much longer.

Similarly, malevolent entities (like angry ghosts or demons) bring their negativity with them wherever they roam. Even if there are no physical signs of a haunting, if these beings are around, their bad presence can be felt on the spiritual plane.

However, most cases of bad energy are not this intense or brought about by such horrible means. If you feel like your home is harboring some bad vibes, it's likely because you've inadvertently brought in the negative energy through the course of normal life.

Assuming you're not a hermit, encountering strife and negativity is unavoidable. Whether someone is rude to you at work or a stranger cuts in line at the grocery store, these small instances of negativity add up, even if they seem insignificant at the time.

When you bring this energy back into your home with you day after day, it can really start to affect both your mental and physical state.

How Does Smudging Banish Bad Energy?

Smudging is a practice that can be found in cultures across time and location. At its most basic, smudging is simply a ceremony where herbs are burnt to achieve purification of some sort. Some people smudge to bless a new home and others smudge to drive out spirits. What ties all of these together is the purifying power of smoke.

Smoke is associated with the element of air, which itself is associated with lightness, purification, and new life. So it's no wonder that witches and non-witches alike turn to this ancient practice for banishing negativity.

The most commonly used herb for smudging is sage, and it's what we'll be using in our banishment ritual. However, other herbs can be used for different purposes—for example, rosemary is a good choice if you're looking to cultivate an aura of romance in your home.

Smudging Ritual for Banishment

This ritual requires the ceremonial burning of herbs, so be sure to take all the necessary precautions to keep you and your home safe!

Items Needed:

- Sage leaves
- Fireproof bowl
- Matches or a lighter

Begin by clearing your ritual space—you'll need to move around quite a bit, so make sure nothing is obstructing your ability to do so. If you have a specific room that you want to banish bad energy from, you can perform this spell in there. If you're looking to cleanse your house entirely, I suggest performing it in the living room.

Stand in the center of the room, raise your hands above your head, and repeat this:

By my will, this place is a beacon of goodwill and positivity. Spirits and energies of negativity are no longer welcome here.

Place your sage leaves in the fireproof bowl and very carefully light them. Allow them to start smoking steadily before moving on to the next step.

When you're ready, say this:

The power of sage banishes. The power of smoke banishes. Through the sacred power of the air, all ill will vanishes.

At this point, you should begin moving around the room to help evenly distribute the smoke. If there's room, I suggest walking a counterclockwise circle (another symbol of banishment) around the perimeter of the room.

As you walk, repeat this softly to yourself:

The smoke cleanses all it touches. No negativity enters, no negativity remains.

Once you're satisfied, carefully place your bowl at the center of the room. Now move to the northernmost point.

Make an "X" with your arms (left arm over right arm), and in a commanding voice repeat this:

Spirits of the north, hear me. Those that mean me harm must leave this place. You are no longer welcome here.

Now, move to the west and repeat what you just said (substituting "west" for "north").

Repeat this process at the south and east as well.

Finally, return to the center of your circle. Reach your right hand high above your head, and then bring it down so that it touches the ground.

Say this:

As above, so below this place is sealed. No bad energy may linger. So mote it be.

At this point, the ritual is over. However, you can smudge the other rooms in your home if you'd like. Simply reignite your sage leaves and walk around the other areas of your house.

As you walk, repeat what you said before:

The smoke cleanses all it touches. No negativity enters, no negativity remains.

Once you're completely finished with the sage, be sure that it is no longer burning. The ashes and any remaining leaves should be disposed of outdoors.

CHAPTER 9: GUARDIAN ANGEL GUIDED MEDITATION

Communicating with spirits on another astral plane is a practice that appears in many religions, witchcraft included. These beings go by many different names—spirit guide, familiar, ascended master, etc.—but in this book we're going to view them as guardian angels.

I do this because I find it's the easiest introduction into the world of spirit communication. Angels are a figure that most people already have a passing familiarity with and associate with safety and goodness, which makes approaching them a bit less intimidating.

In this chapter, I'll be taking a look at what guardian angels are and how they relate to the aims of white magick. Finally, I'll end things with an invocation you can use to contact your guardian angel directly.

What is a Guardian Angel?

The physical world we see around us with our eyes doesn't tell the complete story of the universe. There are other planes of existence operating on higher energy frequencies that are imperceptible to humans most of the time.

However, through magick and guided meditation, we can, for a short time, access these exciting, new planes of existence. And just like in the physical world, there are sentient, intelligent beings that populate these planes.

While not all of these spiritual or astral beings can be considered friendly to humans, the majority of them are—and they are ready and willing to share wisdom, guidance, and protection with us.

For our purposes, we're going to conceptualize these benevolent beings as guardian angels. Theirs is an existence that lies beyond the bounds of human understanding, so we would be wise to listen carefully to what they have to say.

How Can a Guardian Angel Help Me?

Guardian angels, like the name implies, are protectors of those they watch over. You can call upon them for safety during special occasions, like a long trip. But you can also ask them to watch over you day to day, subtly influencing the flow of life to ensure you're safe and cared for.

Additionally, guardian angels can be a deep well of insight for both spiritual and practical matters. They are ready to offer guidance about problems or obstacles you're encountering, as well as knowledge about how to cultivate a genuine, lasting sense of inner peace within yourself.

Guardian Angel Meditation Steps

Now, I'm going to show you a simple meditation exercise that will help you access your own personal guardian angel. Whether you want to petition for protection or ask questions about a problem you're having, this ritual will help put you in contact with this spiritual guide.

Items Needed:

- One white or golden candle
- Matches or a lighter

To begin, set aside a time and place where you won't be bothered. Meditation requires concentration, so you need to find somewhere quiet and peaceful to help cultivate that mindset.

Traditionally, meditation is performed sitting cross-legged on the floor, but feel free to modify this position with a chair or other equipment if it's more comfortable for you—clearing your mind of physical distractions is of the utmost importance. That being said, I don't recommend trying to meditate while standing for safety reasons.

Begin by lighting the candle on a table or the floor in front of you.

Then, recite this short prayer of protection:

As I travel the astral realm and seek guidance from the ascended beings, I clothe my spiritual body in goodness and light. No beings of ill will may cross my path or harm my psyche. The flames of protection surround me.

Now, close your eyes and begin to slow your breathing. At this point, you should be focused on clearing your mind of all thought. All worries and concerns begin to slip away until nothing remains.

You're now ready to enter the fully meditative state. To do this, begin to number your breaths. Begin with number ten and count down to one. With each number, feel yourself slipping even deeper into a blank, empty state. When you reach number one, you should be fully within the spiritual realms of your mind.

Once you reach this point, look around you—all you should see is blackness. Without fear or hesitation, imagine yourself walking forward in the blackness. With each step you take, an object becomes clearer on the dark horizon. As you get closer, you begin to see that it is a door. This is your portal to the astral realm.

Step right up to this door and try to visualize it as clearly as you can. What does it look like—is it simple? Ornate? What material is it made out of? What color is the door? Reach out and place your hand on it—what texture do you feel? Is it warm? Cool?

There is no right answer to these questions—what you see and experience will vary depending on your own personal disposition and subconscious. What's important is that you experience the situation with as much detail as possible.

Now for the moment of truth—reach out your hand to the doorknob, turn it, open the door, and walk through.

You're now standing in a room that's filled with brilliant bright light. There is no need to be afraid, for this is a place of goodness and protection. Standing across the room from you is a figure—this is your guardian angel.

Walk over, and as with the door, do your best to visualize the angel in complete detail. What are they wearing? What does their face look like? What immediate impressions to you perceive about them?

To begin communicating with your guardian angel, use your thoughts—human language is of little use in the astral realm. If you are looking for protection in the physical world, now is the time to ask for it. Or, if you have questions or fears about a problem you're facing, this is when you would lay that all out.

Once you're done, allow some time for your angel to respond. They may choose to speak clearly and directly with you, but oftentimes their messages come to you in symbols and representations that can only be sorted out by your subconscious. So, do your best to remember as much of the experience as possible, but don't worry if the meaning of the message isn't immediately clear to you.

When you're ready to complete this meditation, first take a moment to thank your guardian angel. Then, turn around, open the door once again, and step back out into the darkness.

As you begin to walk back, it's time to return your consciousness back to normal. Begin numbering your breaths again, but this time start with one and move upward towards ten. With each number, your mind slowly resurfaces in the physical world. When you reach ten, open your eyes.

Once your meditation session is over, take some time to think about what your guardian angel told you. I find that I often need to sleep on the message to truly appreciate its content, but it doesn't hurt to think about it immediately afterward to help cement it in your mind.

Be sure to safely extinguish your candle once you're done.

Your guardian angel can be visited whenever you have the time or the desire, so don't be afraid to be in close contact with them. They are a source of wisdom and protection that won't soon run dry.

If you'd like to know more about entering the astral realm and communicating with spiritual beings, I highly recommend my book *Fast Astral Projection for Beginners*. It contains a much more in-depth look at how to reach these heightened planes of existence and commune with the spiritual guides that reside there.

CHAPTER 10: HEX BREAKING SPELL

Sometimes things in our lives go wrong and there's no simple explanation for them—we simply have to learn to accept the fact that sometimes the universe feels indifferent to us. However, there are other times when your bad luck might seem random but is actually the result of a magickal attack.

In this chapter, I'm going to take a look at hexes (or curses). This type of black magick is meant to make the recipient's life miserable and can lead to both spiritual or physical harm. I'll show you how to determine if you are the victim of a hex, as well as a ritual that will help break a spell that someone has maliciously placed upon you.

What is a Hex?

"Hex" is one of those words that can be tricky to pin down.

In some witchcraft traditions, all types of magick are referred to as hexes—everything from love spells to money magick. However, it would be ridiculous to say that all of these hexes are bad and need to be broken. This is not the kind of hex I'm referring to in this book.

When used as a negative term, "hex" is another word that can be used for to mean "curse"—this is what I'm speaking of when I talk about breaking a hex. Like I mentioned earlier, this is a type of magick meant to do spiritual or physical harm to the recipient.

There is no one particular way that someone can place a hex on you. Praying to a vengeful God or Goddess is one way to do it, but others might place a curse on a personal object of yours or draw a sigil to hex you.

What ties all of these practices together under the umbrella term of "hex" is the intention behind the magick. In all of these cases, the purpose of the spell is to generate negative energy and direct it at a specific person.

How Can You Tell if You've Been Hexed?

It can be difficult to determine whether or not you have actually been hexed. As I said before, sometimes the universe just sends bad luck your way for no discernible reason.

Some of the most common forms of hexing involve your personal life—money and relationships. If you find yourself struggling with either money or love and all of these problems seem completely out of the blue, there's a chance you are being hexed.

Some other common targets of hexes include health and beauty. Any unexplained negative changes to your appearance or overall level of health could be indicators of a curse or hex.

Most hexes come about because of a desire for revenge. Is there anyone in your past that you have wronged? Or anyone who thinks you have wronged them even if you didn't actually do it?

If you can answer yes to either of those questions and you're experiencing the above symptoms, there is a possibility that a hex has been placed on you.

Ritual for Breaking a Hex

Luckily, you don't simply have to suffer through a hex. There are magickal actions you can take to break their hold over you.

This is especially true if you're the unfair recipient of one. If you've genuinely wronged the person hexing you, it's a bit more complicated. Breaking the hex before it runs its course is possible, but only if the universe thinks you have learned your lesson. If you're unapologetic for your actions, it's unlikely that the following ritual will do you any good.

Items Needed:

- Jasmine essential oil
- Mirror (the bigger the better)
- Large Black Candle
- Lighter or matches
- Ceremonial knife

This hex-breaking ritual should be performed on the night of a dark (or new) moon—when it's completely covered by darkness in the night sky. This is the time of month when the powers of banishment and spell-breaking are at their highest.

Before the spell begins, you'll want to take a ritual cleansing bath. Fill your tub and place three drops of jasmine essential oil into the water. Jasmine corresponds strongly to peace, serenity, and calmness.

As you do this, repeat the following:

I purify the water so that it may purify my being. Let it wash my body and soul clean.

After this, you can bathe normally or simply take a symbolic dip in the tub.

To begin the ritual, clear your space and place the mirror at the southernmost point, facing outwards. During the course of this ritual, the mirror will be blessed to reflect not only light, but spiritual negativity and malice as well.

Once everything has been arranged, stand at the center of your space, close your eyes, and repeat the following:

I am beset by magickal warfare. I summon the spirits of goodwill to come to my aid. Within the sacred ring we will break the hex.

Now, very carefully use your ceremonial knife to carve a hex-breaking symbol into the body of your black candle. Begin by drawing a circle on it. Now, starting at the top of the circle, draw a straight line down to the center of the circle. To complete the sigil, carve three diverging straight lines from the center down to the bottom part of the circle.

Once this is complete, light the candle and say this:

I conjure the light of banishment. I charge this flame with the power of the sigil to protect everything its light touches.

Next, return to your outward-facing mirror.

Hold the candle over it and repeat this blessing:

O sacred mirror, protect me from the slings and arrows of magickal malice. As the negativity draws close to me, may you reflect it back out safely away from myself and all humankind. I bless you with the power of banishment.

Starting from where you're standing by the mirror, begin to walk a counterclockwise circle around your space three times while still holding the candle.

During the first rotation, say this:

I bind the powers that seek me.

During the second rotation, this:

I control the powers that seek me.

On the final rotation, say this in a commanding voice:

I break the powers that seek me. So mote it be.

Quickly extinguish your candle, but do not move until the wick has finished smoking. Once this happens, the ritual is officially over.

Afterwards, you'll want to keep your candle stored safely until the next dark moon— at which point you should bury it in the ground.

During the three evenings immediately after the hex–breaking ritual, keep the mirror in your bedroom, still facing away from you (preferably towards a window).

If you're still experiencing bad luck after this ritual, there is a good chance you were not the recipient of a hex. However, nothing bad will come about for performing this ritual when it's not needed.

CHAPTER 11: WHITE MAGICK FRIENDSHIP SPELL

So far in this book I've shown you plenty of ways to defend yourself against negative forces in your life, but there is so much more to white magick than just protection! It's about actively cultivating goodness and joy just as much as it's about shielding ourselves against the bad.

In this chapter, I'm going to show you a spell that will help you bring friendship into your life. Whether you're looking to meet new people or want to strengthen and deepen your existing friendships, you can do both with the power of magick!

What Are the Symbols of Friendship in White Magick?

Friendship is a broad concept that has many different correspondences and symbols. For this spell, I've chosen something that I think fits very nicely with the idea of friendship and white magick—flowers!

Like an old friend, flowers brighten your day when you see them. Plus, they are a powerful symbol of life and vitality, which are two important concepts in white magick. In this spell, you'll be blessing and arranging your own friendship bouquet, but before we get to the steps involved, let's take a closer look at the flowers you'll be using.

First up, you'll need carnations. While this stunning flower comes in many different shades, I recommend using light pink. All hues of red represent a connection between human beings, but unlike dark or bright red, which commonly symbolizes romantic love, a nice, light pink is perfect for friendly affection.

Next on the list is dandelion. While most people might think of these as a pesky weed, in witchcraft, dandelion blossoms represent honesty and mutual respect— both of which are important to a healthy friendship.

The forget-me-not is a small but visually stunning blossom—its bright hues of blue or purple make it a flower that stands out from the crowd. Magickally speaking, forget-me-nots are highly associated with memory (which you could probably guess from the name). Within the context of this friendship spell, they're meant to cultivate fond memories with your friends.

The final flower in our bouquet is lavender—which is associated with communicating with the spirit world. By including it in this arrangement, you can be sure that your guardian angel and other spirit guides are adding their own positive energies into your friendship.

The Friendship Ritual

Items Needed:

- Carnation
- Dandelion
- Forget-Me-Not
- Lavender
- Vase (to hold the flowers)
- Water (in another container)

Please note: the exact number of each type of flower can vary depending on personal preference and availability. As long as all four flowers are represented in your bouquet, you'll experience their magickal effects.

To begin, stand in the center of your space and raise your palms above your head while you say this:

I call all spirits of goodwill and friendship into this place. Let us enjoy the company of one another while we make merry magick.

Now, pour the water from its original container into the vase you'll be using for the flowers. Be sure to measure ahead of time to make sure the vase won't overflow when the flowers are placed in it.

After you've poured, repeat this prayer to the Goddess:

Great Mother Goddess, origin of all friendship and love, bless this water that it may nourish these blossoms. As they grow, may my relationships grow too.

Next, take your carnations and hold them above the vase.

While you do this, say:

I bless these carnations with the magick of friendship. May they draw in kind, caring people.

Place the carnations in the vase and then pick up the dandelions.

Their blessing goes like this:

I bless these dandelions with the magick of friendship. May they draw in honorable people with a respect for others.

After placing them in the vase, you should pick up the forget-me-nots next.

While you hold them, say:

I bless these forget-me-nots with the magick of friendship. May they draw in good times and fond memories with unforgettable friends.

They too should now go in the vase.

Finally, pick up the lavender and say:

I bless this lavender with the magick of friendship. May it draw in the blessings of the spirit world on all my friendships.

To complete the ritual, carefully pick up the vase and give it one final blessing:

The beauty of these flowers is enhanced by their mingling. May my life be similarly enriched as I forge relationships with those around me. So mote it be.

Once the spell is done, there are a few things you can do with your bouquet.

The most obvious choice is to leave the bouquet in your home to help surround yourself with the positive spiritual energy it is drawing in. Be sure to water and care for it just as you would non-magickal flowers. And take care to dispose of the flowers respectfully outdoors when they begin to wilt.

However, since this is a friendship bouquet, you could also gift the flowers to a friend you'd like to become closer with. It makes for a thoughtful, beautiful gift that will also enhance their life spiritually and magickally.

CHAPTER 12: EMOTIONAL HEALING RITUAL

Although physical wounds may heal over time, the emotional scars they bring with them can last much longer. While there is nothing, magickal or otherwise, that can help you immediately and instantly "get over" trauma in your past, white magick can provide comfort and perspective during the healing process.

The ritual found in this chapter is all about processing one or more painful moments in your past and learning how to move forward with intention on a restorative, life-affirming path.

I'll be honest, this ritual can be tough to perform—it will require you to bring up some painful memories. However, the purpose of this is not to cause harm by dredging up the past, but rather, it's about bringing your pain to the surface so that you can release yourself from its pervasive power.

What Does This Spell Do?

I've crafted this ritual in such a way that it could apply to any number of different situations. You'll find parts in the spell where you'll be asked to speak about the specific context that you're coming from.

Whether you've had a bad breakup, lost a loved one, or something worse, the point of this ritual is to heal emotional wounds of any kind. Or rather, it's about beginning or reaffirming the healing process—actual healing takes much longer than the length of a spell.

Within the ritual, you'll be invoking the Mother aspect of the Triple Goddess. The Triple Goddess is the central female deity within Wicca, and she is personified through three different archetypes, each with their own attributes and strengths—the Maiden, the Mother, and the Crone.

The Mother is a figure of healing and protection—just like our human mothers are. She hurts when her children hurt, and she is always ready to lend compassion and understanding to souls in need. She is a source of pure love in the universe.

The Mother is also associated with the full moon, so I recommend performing this ritual on the night of one, if possible. If your space will allow it, open the windows so that the light of our celestial Mother can influence your magick directly.

How to Perform the Emotional Healing Ritual

Items Needed:

- 1 black candle
- 1 white candle
- Matches or a lighter
- Silver ribbon (long enough to tie around the white candle)

To begin, clear your space and sit in the middle of it. For the first few moments, take some time to meditate on the painful event(s) in your past. This may not feel comfortable, but it's important to have them in the forefront of your mind. You can't release what you don't acknowledge.

When you're ready, stand with your palms above your head and give this invocation to the Triple Goddess:

Great Triple Goddess, most compassionate Mother, I call upon you this night. The chains of my past bind me, but I am ready for freedom. Lend me your love and your power that I may move forward on the path of healing from [here is where you speak about your specific problem]. Show me the road to restoration. So mote it be.

Now, you'll want to light the black candle. This represents your past.

As you light it, say this:

The past may be over, but its presence still lingers. Into this flame I place the hurt, anguish, and grief that has haunted me. I am illuminated by the light of suffering.

Now, using the flame from the black candle, light the white one—which represents your present/future.

As you do, repeat:

The past flows into the present and into the future. I cannot escape what has come before this moment. I acknowledge the events that have led me to this place.

Next, tie the silver ribbon around the white candle. This represents the Triple Goddess/Mother. If you know how to tie a square knot, use it because of its magickal properties. Otherwise, a simple knot will do.

To continue, say this:

Mother of the sky, I pray for your protection. Bind me with your healing love and restore my past wounds to future health.

Turn your attention to the black candle. This is arguably the most important moment in the entire ritual.

Take a deep breath, and when you're ready, say this:

I cannot change the past and the ways it has shaped me. But through the power given to me by the Mother of all witches, I can move forward into a realm of healing where it may not follow. I lay it down and bind the influence that it has held over me. This is where the new path begins. So mote it be.

Immediately after this, extinguish the black candle so that only the white one is left burning.

Take some time to collect your thoughts, and then say this last prayer to the Triple Goddess:

Most radiant Mother, your presence has been made known here tonight. I will repay the love you have shown me with love towards all of your creatures. Bless me and protect me as I move forward into light. Blessed be.

To end the ritual, extinguish your white candle.

After the ritual is over, keep your white candle in your home and burn it daily until it is completely gone. Your black candle should be disposed of outdoors. Ideally, it should be buried. At the very least it should be disposed of respectfully—even though the past is painful, you do want to honor the fact that it shaped you into the stronger, more resilient person that you are today.

CHAPTER 13: FOLLOW THE LIGHT

Magick is about improving not only your life but the lives of others as well. And I hope that by reading this book, you've become better equipped to do so. Learning how to tap into the healing, compassionate power of the universe, no matter how small your attempt may be, spreads love and joy and makes the world a better place.

It's also my hope that learning about white magick has inspired you to treat yourself with more respect and kindness. You are worthy of the healing you seek. You are worthy of the harmony and prosperity you want in your life. And you alone have the power within you to makes those dreams a reality.

I would be extremely grateful for an honest review of the book. I want to provide my readers with spells and magickal rituals that are important and useful to them, and receiving your feedback is one way I can better serve you.

Blessed Be,

Didi

CHAPTER 14: READ MORE FROM DIDI CLARKE

Forbidden Wiccan Spells: Magick for Love and Power (Vol. 1)

Enchant your way to romance with these Wiccan love spells! Become a master of power magick! Learn all this and much more with this original spell book from Didi Clarke!

Whether you're trying to seduce that special someone or want to show others who's the boss, *Forbidden Wiccan Spells: Magick for Love and Power* has something for everyone. With each chapter, you'll find authentic Wiccan magic that will help you unlock your dreams in love and life!

What You'll Find

Within the pages of *Magick for Love and Power*, you'll find one-of-a-kind spells written and tested by Didi Clarke herself—you won't find books on witchcraft like this anywhere else!

If you're new to Wicca, never fear—this book uses a wicca for beginners approach. The spells are explained thoroughly, and each one comes with a detailed item list and step-by-step directions.

And there's plenty for more experienced witches too. These unique magick rituals will enhance your skills and help you tap into the full potential of love and power! In this book, you'll find a wide variety of magickal practices to explore, including:

- Herbal Magick
- Candle Magick
- Mantra Magick
- Elemental Magick

Are you ready to spice up your life with love spells?

Love is a powerful force, and when you combine it with the power of witchcraft, the results can be truly magickal! In *Magick for Love and Power*, you'll get access to genuine spells and rituals that will help you attract romance into your life and keep the flames of love burning for years to come!

These love spells include:

- Flame gazing to find your true love
- Mantras to keep your partner faithful
- Potions to repair a damaged relationship
- And much more!

Are you ready to harness the strength of power magick?

These power spells are here to change your life for the better. Whether you want to be more assertive at work or tap into the power of the Spirits, this magick will leave you feeling confident and strong!

Here are some of the power spells you'll find in this complete book of witchcraft:

- Amulets for persuasive power
- Rituals for fame
- Incantations for dominance
- Many more!

Learn the Art of Love Magick and Power Magick Today!

Unlock the secrets of witchcraft within the pages of this Wiccan book of shadows written for those seeking love and power! If you're ready to take control and live your best life, read *Magick for Love and Power* today!

Forbidden Wiccan Spells: Magick for Wealth and Prosperity (Vol. 2)

Find true prosperity with these original money spells from Didi Clarke!

Are you ready to embrace the bounty of the Spirit world? Then this is the book for you! *Forbidden Wiccan Spells: Magick for Wealth and Prosperity* lays out everything you need to know in order to master the art of prosperity magick.

What You'll Find

Within the pages of *FWS: Magick for Wealth and Prosperity*, you'll find never-before-seen money spells that will help put you on the right track for financial success. From herbal magick to incantations, the rituals in this book teach you a wide variety of Wiccan magick—it's perfect for everyone from the complete beginner to the seasoned witch!

These spells include:

- A fire incantation for financial windfall
- An herbal sachet for business success
- Mantras for material prosperity
- Crystal blessings for attracting wealthy people
- And much more!

Are You Ready to Transform Your Life With Money Magick?

These spells won't make you a millionaire overnight—nothing can do that—but that doesn't mean you can't seek help from the Spirit world for money matters! This misunderstood but incredibly effective branch of magick has helped countless witches, Wiccans, and other spiritually minded people take charge of their finances in amazing ways.

Explore These Powerful Spells Today!

Each of these rituals has been written and tested by Didi Clarke herself. They're presented in an easy-to-read, step-by-step format and include a detailed item list and suggestions for achieving maximum potency. What are you waiting for? Embrace the wealth of the Universe today with *FWS: Magick for Wealth and Prosperity*!

By Didi Clarke

Forbidden Wiccan Spells: Dark Goddess Magick (Vol. 3)

Darkness isn't a place of evil—it's a creative force for good that empowers Wiccans and Witches just like you! If you want to learn never-before-seen invocations, spells, and rituals that honor powerful Goddesses, this is the book for you!

Forbidden Wiccan Spells: Dark Goddess Magick explores the many Goddesses associated with darkness—Goddesses of the moon, of sleep, of dreams, and yes, even of death. For too long, those afraid of divine feminine power have told us that these Goddesses are "demons" or "monsters" or practitioners of "black magick." But Didi Clarke is here to set the record straight. These divine beings are powerful allies for any witch that approaches them with a clean heart and pure will.

Within the pages of *FWS: Dark Goddess Magick*, you'll find twelve completely original invocations that have been written and performed by Didi herself. In addition to popular Goddesses like Hecate (Goddess of the dead) and Freyja (Goddess of war), you'll find rituals involving lesser-known dark Goddesses like:
- Breksta (Goddess of dreams)
- Oya (Goddess of storms)
- Selene (Goddess of the moon)
- And many more!

Each chapter provides an easy-to-understand history of a particular Goddess, as well as correspondences associated with her. Next, you'll find an item list and step-by-step instructions for a ritual invoking one of these powerful beings. These rituals touch on many different elements of the Craft and include:
- Protection of your home
- Prophetic dreams
- Developing magickal abilities
- Communing with the dead
- Wiccan candle magick
- Wiccan herb magick
- Wiccan crystal magick
- Much more!

Whether you're looking for a book about Wicca for beginners or are a seasoned witch, whether you're a solitary witch or work with a coven, FWS: Dark Goddess Magick has something for you. It's a great addition to your spell book or your book of shadows! Embrace the power of the dark Goddess within and read it today!

Forbidden Wiccan Spells: Tarot Cards and Psychic Development Rituals (Vol. 4)

Are you ready to master the skills it takes to become a world-class tarot card reader? Are you looking for proven rituals and techniques that will enhance your psychic development?

Forbidden Wiccan Spells: Tarot Cards and Psychic Development Rituals has the answers you're looking for!

Psychic development and the art divination are two of the most misunderstood Spiritual practices out there. But despite the stereotypes, these tools are used every day by rational, ordinary people trying to make better decisions and improve their lives.

In this book, Didi Clarke provides you with everything you need to start transforming your own life with the wisdom of the psychic realm!

What You'll Find

Within the pages of *FWS: Tarot Cards and Psychic Development Rituals*, you'll find a comprehensive breakdown of everything you need to become a confident, insightful tarot card reader. From card meanings to developing your own reading style, this book is perfect for beginners or experienced readers who want a refresher course.

In addition to this tarot handbook, you'll also find completely original spells and rituals meant to enhance your psychic abilities. Whether you want to get better at dream interpretation, reading tea leaves, or anything between, these magickal rituals will help you harness the power of the Spirit world to reach that goal!

By Didi Clarke

Unlock The Future With Tarot Card Readings

Tarot cards are by far one of the most popular forms of divination available. Unfortunately, becoming a proficient reader can seem like an uphill battle—but it doesn't have to be like that!

Within the pages of *FWS: Tarot Cards and Psychic Development Rituals*, Didi Clarke addresses the most important things every tarot card reader needs to know, including:

- Card meanings for all 78 cards
- Major themes of the four minor arcana suits
- Choosing the right card spread
- Memorizing meanings vs. intuitive reading
- Identifying relationships and themes across cards

Hone Your Divination Skills With Psychic Development

Tarot is a fantastic tool, but there is so much more to explore in the world of divination too!

If you're ready to expand your psychic abilities in more ways than one, these spells and rituals should leave you feeling insightful and powerful. The rituals include:

- Invoking Gods of prophecy
- Herbal magick to aid dream interpretation
- Automatic writing
- Meditation for encountering spirit guides
- Candle magick for finding lost objects

Achieve Your Full Spiritual Potential Today!

If you're ready to unlock the secrets of the Spirit world through divination of any kind, the time is now! *FWS: Tarot Cards and Psychic Development Rituals* has all the tools you need to become the master of your own life. Read it today!

Don't forget to sign up for my mailing list and receive your free color magick correspondence chart by following the link below!

https://mailchi.mp/01863952b9ff/didi-clarke-mailing-list

Printed in Great Britain
by Amazon